nderer King

The Wanderer King

poems

Theodore Deppe

For Gail Dunn,
With all best wishes —
looking forward to
meeting you in
Springfield This fall —

Theodore Deppe

ALICE JAMES BOOKS
FARMINGTON, MAINE

Cover art by Derek Hill. *Tory Island from Tor More* is reproduced by
permission of the painter and the Ulster Museum, Belfast, Northern Ireland.
Author photo by Michael McAndrews,
reprinted with permission of *The Hartford Courant.*
Cover and text design by Charles Casey Martin.

Alice James Books gratefully acknowledges support from
the University of Maine at Farmington and the Massachusetts Cultural
Council, a state agency whose funds are recommended
by the Governor and appropriated by the State Legislature.

Alice James Books are published by
The Alice James Poetry Cooperative, Inc.
University of Maine at Farmington
98 Main Street
Farmington, ME 04938

I wish to thank the National Endowment for the Arts for a grant that
helped give me time to write some of these poems. I am also grateful to
the Vermont Studio Center for a full fellowship that enabled me to work
on this book.

Many thanks to the following people who have offered suggestions and
provided encouragement during the writing of these poems: Betsy Sholl,
Bob Cording, Debra Kowalski, Bob Kowalski. I am very grateful for
manuscript critiques by Jean Amaral, Doug Anderson, Sue Cowing,
Stephen Dunn, Rita Gabis, Jeff Harrison, Gray Jacobik, Denny Lynn,
Rennie McQuilkin, Marilyn Nelson, and Carol Potter. Thanks, also, to
members of my writing workshops for their criticism and friendship. My
special thanks to Annie Deppe, who saw these poems first.

ACKNOWLEDGMENTS

Some of the poems in this collection first appeared in the following journals:

Beloit Poetry Journal: "Set Design for the City."
Boulevard: "Jacob Stern, Photographer and AIDS Activist, 13th Precinct Station, Manhattan, January 1, 1994."
Cream City Review: "The Book of God."
Green Mountains Review: "The *Funeral March* of Adolf Wölfli," "The Last Summer of America."
Harper's Magazine: "The *Funeral March* of Adolf Wölfli" (reprinted from *Green Mountains Review*).
Image: "The Wanderer King," "Installation with Angel," "Spiritual Direction."
The Kenyon Review: "The Japanese Deer."
The Louisville Review: "The Paradise of Wings."
The Massachusetts Review: "Admission, Children's Unit."
New Virginia Review: "Days of Heaven," "The Angels of Bloomington," "Children on a Road, Cuernavaca," "Everyday Books and Cafe."
Passages North: "Family Portrait."
Poetry: "Red Pigeons."
Poetry Northwest: "Letter to Suvorin," "Gooseberries."
Southern Poetry Review: "The Russian Greatcoat."

"Admission, Children's Unit," "The Book of God," and "Gooseberries" appeared in *Between the Heartbeats: Poetry and Prose by Nurses,* University of Iowa Press, 1995.

"The Japanese Deer" and "The Book of God" appeared in *This Wood Sang Out,* an anthology supporting The Literacy Project.

*For Annie
and for Caitlin, Peter, and Michael*

CONTENTS

PART ONE   1

Letter to Suvorin   3
Gooseberries   6
The Book of God   8
Red Pigeons   10
Admission, Children's Unit   12
Children on a Road, Cuernavaca   14
The Paradise of Wings   16
Night Voices   17
The Japanese Deer   19

PART TWO   23

Jacob Stern, Photographer and AIDS Activist,
    13th Precinct Station, Manhattan, January 1, 1994   25
Installation with Angel   28
Halfway House   31
The Wish to See Cyclones   32
The Last Summer of America   34
Family Portrait   36
The Russian Greatcoat   38
Days of Heaven   39
Rita Machado   42

PART THREE   45

The *Funeral March* of Adolf Wölfli   47
Falling from the Grand Hotel   50
Set Design for the City   52
The Angels of Bloomington   54

After Reading about an Act of Vandalism in
    Norwich, Connecticut, My Wife and I
    Enter Salvatore Verdi's "Bathtub Grotto"   56
Everyday Books and Cafe   58
Spiritual Direction   60
The Wanderer King   61

Notes   68

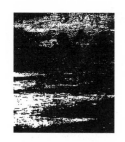

PART
ONE

Letter to Suvorin

Anton Chekhov, Sakhalin Island, off the coast of Siberia

July 11, 1890

Greetings, friend, from the world's end! You were right,
the tea is terrible! We are moored at last off Sakhalin.
Because there's no true harbor we'll sleep on board,

cross the bay of reefs by daylight. Six thousand miles
of floods, thieves, mud and tedium between me
and home—I almost understand

why you say this place doesn't concern us.
On shore, forest fires march down the mountains—
perhaps these flames are eternal, no one in the village

tries to put them out. On deck, the same numbed peace:
women and children, soldiers and manacled convicts
huddle together and try to sleep.

—But even here the weeks pass. It's August now.
I woke at five this morning as I do each day to bells
from St. Vladimir's squat log cabin of a church.

Since the convicts are refused entrance, I, too, stay clear.
I pulled on two pairs of pants for warmth, smoked my pipe
watching the Tartar Straits sunrise, then worked till dark.

I've decided to interview every person on the island.
You say these lifers hold no interest, but on the contrary
I can't stop thinking of them. This morning

I met Mikhail, a man chained two years to a wheelbarrow.
Like so many others, but with his four-year-old, his Nadja,
who's always at his side, even sleeps in his barrow.

And thin Lydia, a twelve-year-old who answered
all my questions, then asked could I afford
a whole rouble to lie with her?

I forced myself last week to watch a whipping.
A doctor like myself examined the man they meant to break,
pronounced him fit for ninety lashes.

The flogger dealt five blows from the left,
five from the right, impassive as a teacher belting a child.
It's not the same, I know, but I kept seeing my father,

how he'd lift the cane above his head, reaching
for more force. I was five. He made me kiss
the rod that taught me justice. I fled the guardhouse,

the whipped man's cries following me down wood sidewalks.
In one yard I saw a rooster tied by its leg,
in another a lock and chain around a pig's neck—

I swear, everything on this island's bolted down.
I climbed to the lighthouse, my favorite spot,
spray breaking over rocks named The Three Murderers,

and along the cliff line the windblown fires
have their own grandeur.
What do you think, is even hell beautiful?

Last night, beneath Bengal lanterns and fireworks,
I dined with Sakhalin's governor high above the village.
The governor spoke on "the golden age of prison care."

My own speech, on building the island's first school,
disappeared in polite applause. A warden
who'd drunk too much French champagne

told of hanging nine men for a single crime:
"There was an entire bouquet hanging in the air."
When the bodies were lifted down

the doctor found one still alive.
Some nights, since he hanged the man
a second time, the warden can't sleep.

How I long to leave this island! Alexey, when I see you next
in Petersburg we will have tea and jam on a silver tray
—how absurdly happy I felt just now, writing that!

Imagine, candlelight on thick preserves,
raspberry or gooseberry, and everything terrible in life
again going on out of sight.

Listen, friend, I need you. Tell me how do we savor
good tea while others suffer? How do we
give thanks for the taste of gooseberries?

Gooseberries

Children's unit, St. Dympna's Hospital

For the first time in weeks, staying up all night
on suicide watch, I find I'm happy.
My job is to pay attention, which I can do

listening to Coltrane on the radio, quietly
so as not to wake Luke, the nine-year-old
just an arm's length away. I scan his homemade quilt

for movement, recalling the girl who years ago
sliced her wrist with a thumbtack
while her bedside nurse watched but couldn't see.

Grateful for these few hours, I read a story by Chekhov
in which Ivan's brother achieved his life's goal—
tasting gooseberries grown on his own land.

Yet the story is really about Ivan, how he sees
his brother's happiness ignores the grief of others.
How many satisfied, happy people

there really are! he thinks. *What a suffocating force it is!*
Luke wakes from a nightmare of his father
that for a minute doesn't stop even after he sits up;

but he's exhausted, falls back to sleep,
and I return to my chair, the open volume of Chekhov
like a small tent before the dark corridor.

When Luke was three, his father hit him
with a baseball bat, left him comatose for a month.
On his sixth birthday, Luke slashed his forearm, prayed

most of the night that he would die. Angels
with red wings corner him now when he is alone.
Last evening in the shower they made him

pummel his face until the aide found him.
I don't want a life that's walled off from such pain,
yet I don't want my old cult of suffering, either.

Tonight I envy what Chekhov, who once traveled
6000 miles to interview prisoners,
tasted years later, the night before his body

was carted back to Moscow in a dirt-green van
marked *Oysters*. Knowing he would die
before his doctor's oxygen arrived

he sent downstairs for champagne—
Such a long time since I've tasted champagne!

The Book of God

St. Dympna's Hospital, 1994

I'm thinking tonight of the three times
Marisol's tried to kill herself before her sixth birthday—

long red suture lines on both arms—
and of the picture she cut from the *Newsweek*

I'd brought to read on break—I still don't know
how she got it—a photo of a crucified girl,

one of several Bosnian children nailed to the doors
of their own homes to frighten the parents away.

For Marisol she hangs there without explanation,
head bent down, black hair falling over jutting ribs.

The single spike through her blue feet
rotates her legs inward, creating a knock-kneed

pigeon-toed schoolgirl of a saint.
Around the tortured girl Marisol taped whole tulips

from the hospital garden. Sacrilege,
my taking down her bedside shrine.

Nothing I said about the photo
troubling the other children made sense:

when I took the picture from her wall
she dug her nails in my wrist, tried to bite my hand.

Only later, and reluctantly, she accepted
the spiral notepad I gave her to write about the girl.

She didn't want words inside but on the cover
she wrote in block letters THE BOOK OF GOD CAME BACK

AS A SMALL GIRL. On each page
she drew pictures she couldn't talk about.

Red Pigeons

Josh wakes each morning between 2 & 3,
    won't stop crying as the rest of the unit
        tries to sleep. I'd sedate him

but the doctor wants this ten-year-old
    evaluated without meds. All night
        he draws magic marker variations

on his one theme: I call him
    The Master of Red Pigeons.
        Illuminated birds circle

burning tenements in each picture—
    in the one he gave me
        the street's an orange line

slashing toward homes it never reaches:
    row houses rise in multicolored flames,
        each blaze tilted a different angle,

everything wave & roll & ripple of fire
    while smoke spirals up
        in little cyclones.

Just out of reach of the sparks
    brilliant birds ride the updrafts,
        outstretched wings reflecting fire.

For a moment, he makes a song of it.
    Until I look up, until he sees
        that I've looked up, he sings

a few lines about a boy at a burning window
            watching red pigeons. It's almost
                    as if we're playing.

It's almost as if the wooden fire escape
            he's added to the house
                    isn't already burning.

Admission, Children's Unit

Like the story of St. Lawrence that repelled me
when I heard it in high school, how he taught
his disciples to recognize the smell
of sin, then sent them in pairs through the Roman Empire,
separating good from evil, brother from brother.
Scrap of legend I'd forgotten until, interviewing a woman,
I drew my breath in and smelled
her, catching a scent that was there, then not there.

She said her son set fire to his own room,
she'd found him fanning it with a comic, and what
should she have done? Her red hair
was pulled back in a braid, she tugged at its flames,
and what she'd done, it turns out, was hold her son
so her boyfriend could burn him with cigarettes.
The details didn't, of course, come out at first,
but I sensed them. The boy's refusal to take off his shirt.
His letting me, finally, lift it to his shoulders
and examine the six wounds, raised, ashy, second
or third degree, arranged in a cross.

Silence in the room, and then the mother blaming
the boyfriend, blaming the boy himself.
I kept talking to her in a calm voice, straining
for something I thought I smelled beneath
her cheap perfume, a scent—how can I describe this?—
as if something not physical had begun to rot.

I'd like to say all this happened when I first started
to work as a nurse, before I'd learned not to judge
the parents, but this was last week, the mother was crying,
I thought of handing her a box of tissues, and didn't.

When the Romans crucified Lawrence,
he asked Jesus to forgive him for judging others.
He wept on the cross because he smelled his own sin.

Sullen and wordless, the boy got up, brought his mother
the scented, blue Kleenex from my desk,
pressed his head into her side. Bunching
the bottom of her sweatshirt in both hands,
he anchored himself to her. Glared at me.
It took four of us to pry him from his mother's arms.

Children on a Road, Cuernavaca

*The dragon's been driven from heaven and comes
down raging to us.* —Revelations 12:12

There's a shop with wooden coffins
stacked to the ceiling. An old man
scratches the packed dirt yard
with a broom made of twigs.
Beneath the card table where his wife
sells candies, pigeons spook me
with their liquid questions.
I'm walking the rim of the ravine,
trying to find the music
I've heard all evening.
Above the piecemeal shacks
and whitewashed church the moon
is rising larger than at home,
and whispering children appear.
A girl dances barefoot on the road.
The others make a drumming sound
on their thighs while dogs bark
from the roof of the coffin shop.
Even the dust is luminous. A boy leaps
from the shadows, roars like a dragon.
The young ones drum louder,
the dragon circles the girl
and raises his hand for silence.
I watch him tilt his head back
and fill his mouth with gasoline
from a soda bottle. He rolls it
on his tongue, lifts a lighter
to puffy red lips, spits
flames into the dark.
Who taught these children

to breathe fire?
Across the ravine, music
and dozens of flamebursts
as others make the burned air hiss.
Smell of scorched flesh.
Moonlight on a hairless face.
The dragon kisses the girl's hand,
then both come begging.

The Paradise of Wings

My grandfather called it
the Paradise of Wings, a clearing
hidden in blue hills where thousands
of geese gleaned stubbled corn
beside a tapered lake. His favorite walk—
shared with me as a secret—made of that place,
those burnished wings, a sort of gift.

That fall, when flocks funneled above our house,
he'd hoist my sister to his lap
so I could go alone, be his eyes and ears.
I'd wait in a blind of scrub oak, calculate
the time to break from hiding, then whirl
my arms until the low sky rose in a wide arc
to settle out of sight behind the ridge.

One day my sister stumbled from the house,
panic in her face as she ran to me.
Though Grandfather stopped at the front steps
we ran all the way to the valley
I'd sworn to keep secret.
She made me promise
never to leave her alone with him,

told me just enough so that I, too,
feared his hands. Light kept draining
from black water, leaving in its place
an opaque stillness
where geese stood about on shelves of rotting ice
and my sister's hate
was the only living thing in paradise.

Night Voices

St. Dympna's Hospital

On 2 a.m. rounds I hear a mockingbird,
different songs in each room as if my flashlight
played through a huge aviary, the curled backs
and sleeping faces washed in this mish-mash
of come-ons and put-downs, scoldings and sweet-nothings.

Only one patient, retired professor Charles Gardner,
is awake. Wrapped in a flowered robe
he sits in his doorway so the faint hall light
falls on his book which he holds
closed in his lap—"I can't even read Walt now."

He offers to lend me Whitman's Civil War journals
for the shift. Tangled brows rise above kind, defeated eyes.
In the long hospital night, I follow Whitman
through crowded wards where he helps
one man write a letter, brings pudding to another.

In the margin, Gardner's written "The Gospel
According to Walt." He's highlighted the words
*Oscar Wilber wanted me to read from the Bible, asked
"do I enjoy religion"—I said probably not
my dear, in the way you mean.*

Down the hall someone's shouting. I find
"Alpha-and-Omega" Jones, bipolar street musician,
crying out and humming in bed
as his fingers spider chords in the air above him.
I try to quiet him but he's midway

through a medley: he murmurs a few lines
from B.B. King, kicks out
in his one transition, "And Alpha-and-Omega sings,"

hurling himself headlong into the next song.
He pauses long enough to say

living his life is like leaping from a balcony
to a chandelier, swinging above a party,
riding the flames across the room.
He calls this world his "mournful
thousand-and-one RPM heaven."

In his doorway, Charles Gardner—
still dressed in his dead wife's clothes—
doesn't even raise his eyes as I pass.
I catch a hint of Shalimar.
I know I have no words to comfort him.

Back at the nursing station I read Whitman's notes
about a Hoosier volunteer who broke ranks
at Bull Run, scrunched in beneath
a flowering bush he couldn't name,
listened all night as a bird found sounds

for what was bursting in his head.
There were still children's primers stacked in a corner
of the schoolroom-turned-hospital-ward
where Whitman cradled him. Rough
humming kept welling up from the boy's lips.

The Japanese Deer

*For Denny Lynn, who likes to know what's true in
my poems and what's "made up."*

What's true in this is that Luis, not his real name,
sat next to me on the field trip to the Lost Village
because I didn't trust him farther back in the van.
Also true, when we returned to the Children's Unit
he drew me a picture with scented markers
in which rabbit-sized deer leapt through a dangling fence
while a funnel cloud labeled "Hurricane Gloria"
shot apple blossoms through the air.

Luis didn't, however, see the Japanese deer
though I'd told him to watch for twelve-point bucks
the size of fawns. Years ago, before they were loosed
by Gloria, I sometimes fed that herd
at Henry Joy's deer yard, a few miles
from the Lost Village's unmarked logging road.
Hard to say if they still survive in those hills,
tame, miniature deer that ate from the hands of strangers.

I told the kids I'd never been to the Lost Village.
Not true. I think I wanted them to believe
we might get lost finding it, might *have* to get lost,
unnecessary pretense since I led them
unintentionally down a wrong path,
had to double back, follow a cut to a stream
where gold finches flashed their dull fire
beside the ruins of a mill.

Further back, cellar holes like sunken gardens,
foundations reclaimed by blackberries and ferns.
No historical marker here,
only a friend's story of an English deserter
who fled to the wilds of Connecticut
and fathered sixteen children, some lodged now

beneath fiddleheads, the low cemetery walls
unable to hold back the forest.

But what surprised me that day
was the apparition of apple blossoms
seen through the woods, children breaking ranks
and running. I tried to judge the danger:
wind whipped the sweet, heavy scent
of flowers about the orchard, children rode
the lower branches, while dead limbs
creaked in trees unpruned a hundred years.

What's true in this story is that Marisol,
raped repeatedly by her mother's boyfriend,
and Luis, who watched from the hall as his stepfather
stabbed his mother to death—nothing
can change those facts—climbed for a short time
above the brambled understory, outside history,
discovered a fragrant scent on their hands,
shredded more petals, rubbed the smell deep in their skin.

As I drove back roads to the hospital
a few of the girls slept,
apple sprays wilting in their hair.
A white-tailed doe looked up
from the center of the asphalt, froze,
then bounded into the evening woods
before most of the children saw her.
Back on the unit, though,

they were sure they'd seen one of the Japanese deer—
some had seen the whole herd, small as fawns,
watching silently from the shadows.

Now, on my study wall, the drawing Luis gave me:
deer he never saw leap in pairs
through an autumn storm that kicks up
spring flowers, impossible, all of it,
but this is the way he remembers it; this is the truth.

PART
TWO

Jacob Stern, Photographer and AIDS Activist, 13th Precinct Station, Manhattan, January 1, 1994

They want a statement yet confiscate
my film, film that is my statement.
Let them develop those self-portraits
carefully in the forensics darkroom
and I'll have said what I need to say:
something more will rise

from those emulsive baths than mere images
of a sick and naked man covered with lesions
photographing himself in Gramercy Park.
Still, I don't mean to be difficult—
until there are pictures accept these words.
My name is Jacob Stern, and I've never before

been arrested. And though I have no gift for dreams—
cannot in fact recall them most mornings—
I woke last night from a dangerous one,
a sort of challenge I couldn't let pass.
But first I must tell you of my brother
and the photograph he had me take

fifty years ago in Amsterdam.
Perhaps you've seen it, *Life*'s Photo of the Week, 1941,
David striding onto Leidse Straat, naked
except for his shoes, socks, and woolen hat,
and the umbrella he bought in Dover
which lofts above him, unable to shelter

bare skin from gusting rain, so what light there was
glistens on his shoulders and buttocks.
Seeing it for the first time, framed
above my piano, some of my guests laugh:

maybe it's the umbrella, patently unable
to protect him, or maybe, reminded of dreams

in which they, too, walk naked in public,
they're simply glad it happened to David,
not themselves. But don't judge them;
we laughed, too, as David tuned the wireless
to jazz, modeled different outfits,
or lack of them, improvised conversations

with surprised nuns, hookers, Gestapo.
Only by reading *Life*'s short commentary
do my guests learn his protest against
clothes rationing led him to Bergen-Belsen.
He required so little of me.
I wanted to follow him but the photo's

very existence demanded I pocket
my pawnshop Leica, convey the film
to safety. David crosses alone to the Municipal Theater,
the stippled blur rising in the grainy background
where he'll recite his protest speech
as cool rain peppers his skin.

But I promised to tell you the dream: we'd gathered
for Seder when David, still young of course,
calmly stripped and handed his clothes to Father,
then flew slowly down red-carpeted stairs.
Suspended for a moment in the open door,
he turned to me, told me to unaccommodate

myself to this world. I stood in the draft
with my camera, unable to follow.
You must understand, if I've accommodated myself,

as David says, it's been to survive.
Strange to have an older brother
half-a-century younger than me, possessing

a martyr's wisdom I don't know how to use.
In the photo, David strides rapidly away from us,
so we can only imagine the amused crowd
that will gather for his speech,
imagine how the SS man
enters the circle, ready to pistol-whip

my brother whose nakedness almost invites
his violence, but for whatever reason
he holds back—I don't know how I know this
but I do—holds back, removes his coat, drapes it
almost fraternally over David, helps him
by the shoulder to the waiting car.

Once, I followed David by disappearing
in a crowd. Last night, thinking of so many friends,
then and now, who died while we turned away,
I saw how that crowd was a throng of ghosts
and the rules changed:
before I disappear, I will be visible.

Installation with Angel

After Sharon McConnell. Gut, zipper, metal, water,
72"x24"x12"

Annie brings me to see the angel: suspended
from a wire hook in its own corner of the room,
this pale, diaphanous dress made from pig gut,

this shimmering, see-through angel of a dress
floats above a stained aluminum tub.
Part and not part of this installation, it flickers

beyond the portable shrines made from worn suitcases,
the junked armchairs fitted with gold wings—
this gown with its delicate stitches in tissue so thin

that when I breathe on it the garment spins.
On a bench, Annie remembers
how the midwife punctured the caul

on the premature baby of our friend, Corrie:
gauzy as this pig-gut angel, the wet membrane
had sealed in a misformed child,

almost limbless, unable even to gasp for air.
For an hour the midwife breathed for it,
then, with a nod from Corrie, baptized it, let it die.

Strange, armless bird that haunted
those nights in Kentucky—
that year, in our house without running water,

the children wouldn't fall asleep
without our tape of Gregorian chant.
Carrying buckets of spring water from the car

I heard the *Salve Regina* as chimney smoke rose
straight up into a windless sky of stars.
I know we failed there to make each other happy.

Cramped, tiny kitchen with its buckets of water,
icons and candles lighting a house
that was too small—I see that now—

but shining. In the silence
after the plainsong, Annie undressed
for a sponge bath by the cookstove:

the kerosene lamp's watery light
caught the small of her back as she bent
in the white tin basin to wash her feet.

The slightest breath now and the dress
spins again, slow dance above its tub.
I want it to be the angel of second chances.

Annie was with the midwife
while I worked on the Taylor's barn, hammer
echoing against the ridge, me glad in the knowledge

that at the bottom of the hill, in that very old,
freshly painted white bus, Corrie Taylor
was giving birth. *Resurrectum mundi* sang the monks,

resurrection of the world of ten thousand cast-off things,
sunlight trumpeting off shattered windshields.
Two dumped Fords beneath the Taylor's bridge,

eyesores until I saw how they shored the bank.
Night followed night, ice
startled me awake, breaking on the river.

Angel, you wept on our kitchen floor
and nothing I could say or do could comfort you.

Halfway House

A red-haired man sits on his suitcase
ready to go anywhere. Having carried
what he could into the snowy night,
he watches from the sidewalk as fire trucks arrive.

A second, older man shelters a potted lily
in his unzipped coat. The blossoms
will be crushed if he covers them completely
so a few ghostly trumpets blare

silently into the storm.
Headphoned and running in place,
a jogger listens to his own soundtrack
for the burning building

only there aren't any flames—
firefighters glide angrily through unharmed rooms.
I feel guilty and exhilarated, part of a crowd
watching a house that's not on fire.

A woman from the doughnut shop
brings cups of coffee in a cardboard box,
strangers share cigarettes. The jogger's almost
dancing to his music while yellow-suited firefighters

enter and leave the house like goldfish.
Who set this invisible fire? Every light
in the group home blazes into the dark.
When the alarm's turned off the silence pulses.

Snow comes down harder. I almost speak
to the man whose huge hand brushes off the petals
of his doomed lily. How has it happened
I'm one block from home and don't know a soul?

The Wish to See Cyclones

for Lynda Hull (1954–1994)

On video tape you lean into the mike,
your voice more & more Jersey as you recite
those lines about risking everything.
One slim, nervous hand brushes back
newly reddened hair, you close your eyes to read
& the city plunges into radiant night.

So easy to get lost, following you
through Chinatown alleys & hotels,
neon streets & harbors. When it's over,
you raise your glass to us & part the curtain
that's shimmered all night as backdrop:
my last glimpse of you, waving as you vanish.

But I can't shake the feeling I've seen that curtain
years ago, a sheet of thunderclouds
illuminated by 4th of July fireworks.
Tornadoes were sighted in the next town
so a half-hour's program was launched
as one grand finale—splendid, though everything

happened too fast, the mind couldn't sort out
the windblown patterns as they merged into a deafening,
strobe-lit drape through which a twister might rage.
I walked home backwards with my family
applauding the dazzling storm. As now,
at film's end, the audience applauds you.

I play the tape back, watch the light that is not
you, those moving dots that capture how you stressed
each dark syllable & again you build
your luminous city, wanting to leave nothing out:
steam bath, nightclub, chop shop, a few dim stars
above the torched cars & storefront church.

Let's get lost. Why court the brink & then step back?
Sirens somewhere, fragrance of gunpowder
mixed with the scent of hot pavement
as the first fat drops pelted the road.
I climbed the hill with the crowd, carried the small weight
of my youngest son toward dry pajamas,

but I kept looking back, wanting to see a cyclone
burst through the pulsing light.
It's not that simple. All of us cheered, yes,
but hurried toward shelter, seeking that place
where what we love can last a while.
I visited you last winter in Provincetown,

your rented rooms filled with things you treasured:
fine, dwarf roses in the bedroom window
overlooking the sea & beside them the head
of an heirloom doll your mother brought from Poland.
One week earlier you'd overdosed & found
—in that blur of Valium—how much you wanted to survive.

Later, quoting Berryman, you said that the worst thing
that happens to us that does not destroy us is the best thing
that happens to us. Which was where we left it.
Snow was melting, we walked toward town, listened
to the sounds of things rivering in swollen streets
where all that is is once, then rushes on.

The Last Summer of America

In the snapshot I stole from the family album years ago,
it's the last summer of America.

Newly widowed, mid-forties, my grandmother
sits in the shade of a crippled pickup
somewhere in Montana or Wyoming.

From the dry creek where the guest-ranch's truck
broke an axle, it's a three-day walk to the nearest road

so the guide set out by night, following stars north,
hoping to flag a train. Those left behind
shared little gifts: bouquets of wildflowers

quickly withered, whiskey and cigarettes,
and photos of each other—my grandmother

never could recall who took this portrait.
In one version of the story, Death
sized her up, shot a sort of passport photo,

the sun's glare hammering even the shadows.
It was 1941 and, certain the Nazis would invade,

she'd taught herself to drive, abandoned
her victory garden in August, left Boston
to see her country before it fell.

Long convoys of men playing war games,
waving as she passed. Once, she said

she'd set off looking for a new love.
And once, that she'd searched the country
for her husband, a man she'd hated so long

she couldn't stop looking for him.
She said he dominated any space he moved through,

controlled each situation. "He wasn't capable
of getting lost!" Everything that August
seen for the first and final time,

windows flaring up and vanishing along a river,
gulls rising above an inland sea, a storm

sweeping black hills. She looks almost at home,
lost in the heart of America.
It's the only photo I've seen in which she's smiling.

Family Portrait

1955, at the edge of memory,
two uncles argued at my Aunt Betsy's wedding.
I thought Uncle Ced, the tall one, might kill
his brother Robert, but they made up,
left the reception arm-in-arm,
wove across the dark lawn.

It was night, they entered the fog, and when we followed
we found black and white wedding clothes
hanging from branches near the beach.
Best of all, their underwear folded neatly
on an upturned rowboat. Close my eyes
and I still hear Mother calling

as we take off down the beach,
hoping to catch a glimpse of naked uncles.
We knew the bay was out of bounds
but realized suddenly they were out there,
hidden in the fog, no way to find them.
Grownups came, organized a search party.

Sometimes it seems our family is one great
party, a jazz band and lots of drinks,
someone quarreling or talking secretly,
and then the whole whirling scene
gets too much, the wheel gathers speed
and flings one of us outside the circle—

someone's lost again, someone's calling for help
and no one hears. How long was it
before my uncles appeared
halfway down the beach, clutching
a single red towel in front of them
as if joined at the hip?

I remember that procession from the cove,
Aunt Betsy calling for the photographer
as she bunched the hem of her dress
with both hands and marched
beside her naked brothers.
The neighbor's Labs licked at their legs

as we filed back to the beach house
whose lights floated above us in the shifting dark.
In the photo, both brothers hide
behind their towel but manage to wave
at the camera with their free hands.
I can't remember Aunt Betsy's wedding

earlier that day, can't recall her Scotsman
who briefly entered our lives
before he, too, lost his footing and disappeared.
What stands out now is the moment the whole dance
halts before my uncles' wedding clothes,
the two men vanishing in the trees,

and all of us treading in place in that darkness,
marking our spot by an upturned boat.

The Russian Greatcoat

While my children swim off the breakwater,
while my wife sleeps beside me in the sun,
I recall how you once said you knew
a sure way to paradise or hell.
Years ago, you stood on the Covington bridge,
demanded I throw my coat into the Ohio—
my five dollar "Russian greatcoat,"
my "Dostoevsky coat," with no explanations,
simply because you asked.

From that height, the man-sized coat fell
in slow motion, floated briefly,
one sinking arm bent at the elbow.
At first, I evade the question when my wife asks,
as if just thinking of you were an act of betrayal.
The cigarette I shared with you above the river.
Our entrance into the city, your thin black coat
around our shoulders. Sometimes I can go
weeks without remembering.

Days of Heaven

In my only letter from my brother
        it's 1976, he's dropped out of Oberlin
and is walking west across Canada
        "because I want to skip the celebration."

The way David tells it, he never tried out
        to be an extra in *Days of Heaven;*
he'd washed his hair in some public library sink
        and was reading Heidegger while he shaved,

when Terence Malick came in to use the john.
        Before David finished washing up
Malick offered him a bit part as a drifter,
        "shameless typecasting" my brother wrote,

though by the time of the film's release
        he was in the Mission Street hotel
where I think he still lives, composing on sax.
        I've never heard him play,

but once I dreamed I took the next room,
        listened through the thin wall
to a sound so frightening I wanted
        to tear the Sheetrock apart and save him.

The first time I saw the film I looked for him
        whenever silhouetted migrants
climbed down from freight cars or pitched
        bluish-orange wheat at the horizon.

David's scenes—shot in weird ribbons of light
        twenty minutes or so past sunset—
seem less concerned with human history
        than possible shades of evening clouds.

David joined each day the long
        motor procession to the Hutterite fields,
rehearsed his scenes and then clowned
        with the cast in deepening wheat,

waiting for slant light to hammer everything
        with that gilt sheen for which Malick's
often faulted—"the film's too
        beautiful." Even if it's true,

I'm haunted as frame by frame
        the light grows stranger and more stunning
while the characters separate themselves
        from paradise, and know it.

When David last appears, he's waving his coat
        at a wheat fire, part of a ragged line
of farm hands trying to beat down the flames
        that will cut short their season's work.

I don't know if the migrants will get paid
        or where they'll go—follow the harvest
north I guess. Maybe David's character
        will stick it out another season.

But when I'm in my "brother mood,"
        lugging about what I don't understand
through my daily rounds, I sometimes watch
        for his brief, sun-and-shadow appearances.

In his battered coat and hat, when he might
        be anyone, he's most himself.
He rides on a freight car roof
        next to some woman—maybe for a few weeks

she got to know him—and though they hold
      hands in his frayed coat pocket
he stares at the last light, its nuanced body,
      wears his solitude like a birthright.

Rita Machado

Strange to be in São Paulo again,
no longer a nun living among the poor
but one of them. I work this garden,
the red carnations I love trimming the edges,
neighboring plots tilting away from me.
I don't know how this will end
or how long I'll keep my vow
to Saint Sobriety. But this is the day-to-day life
I'd longed for: prayer of the small fire,
prayer of the baking of bread
and of its sharing. The children
have found me out, and I'm almost happy.

When I checked out of detox in New York,
I didn't tell anyone where I was going—
I didn't want that lifeline. I guess
that's one more manifestation of warped pride.
Damn right, sister.
Alcoholic ex-nun disappears *perfectly*.
The laundry does a deadman's jig
on this hill angled above factory fires.
Just down the path, the neon shrine
to the Black Virgin guards the ravine
that's been used more than once as body dump.

Tonight I've joined thousands of others
streaming into the city to watch a movie
projected onto the whitewashed wall
of the plastics factory. No foothold, the flow
of whole neighborhoods into the square
keeps us backpedaling, craning
to watch the film flickering above us.
This is the long delayed showing of *Pixote*
for the city's poor. Firecrackers

on the crowd's edge, celebration
and mourning as the Workers' Party honors
Fernando da Silva, slain street kid-turned-actor
who will always be twelve years old,
thirty feet tall, tucking his gun into his belt.

Years ago, when I was Sister Rita,
Hector Babenco told me he wanted
to catch the soul on film. I coaxed
hundreds of homeless children
to screen tests, helped them memorize
the same three lines. When those words
they'd learned by heart were used up,
the camera lingered on their faces,
kept shooting. Such strange auditions,
illiterate street kids trying out to play
themselves. One small girl, Marisa,
couldn't understand why she wasn't chosen—
I ended up just holding and rocking her.

Little soul. Little sister of the broken world.
Are you here tonight? Have you made it
this far? So many restless, batlike
souls flitting across the wall above us.
Two girls wearing phosphorescent bracelets
and headbands clamber onto a tractor truck,
dance together as if their lives
could be lifted up, wholly transcribed into light.
A police helicopter eases down,
bathing us in blue-white glare.
For now, they seem content to film us.
The two girls wave and keep dancing,
litter and dust rising in whirlwinds.
Maybe the camera zooms in for a close-up

before the chopper tilts and rises.
I see us for a moment as they do,
the river of poor, darkness swallowing us
as they angle up for a bird's eye view,
São Paulo a dizzying web of lights
beginning to spin.

I've had nothing to drink tonight
though I'm binging now
on the press and surge of revelers.
Is this why I came back,
to join with this crowd heading home?
True, for a while I just felt lost,
swept up in the outgoing tide,
click and roll of sea rocks
cast up to be ground down.
But when did we become one long wave?
How have we ended up like this—
arms around each other, merged
in these bright streets so thoroughly
as if we'd never again
have to close ourselves off from anyone.

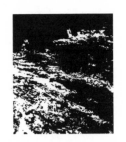

PART
THREE

The *Funeral March* of Adolf Wölfli

From the oral history of Lisa Becker taken in Berne,
Switzerland, 1970.

I found that art would keep him quiet. After breaking
a fellow patient's wrist, he was isolated for years

—I brought him colored pencils and newsprint
and he drew all day or composed music in a system

God revealed to him. For a time he thought he loved me.
For a time my face appeared in every drawing he made.

He wrote the *Santa Lisa Polka* for me, hardly danceable, but
despite the home-made paper trumpet he hummed on, haunting

and mine. He said, once, if I married him, he'd abdicate
his kingdom, write a waltz for me each day.

Strange, then, after he died, to search in vain
through his 8,000 page *Funeral March,* looking

for something—anything—I could play before we buried him.
His masterpiece reached to the ceiling of his cell,

hand-sewn scores in which the music constantly gave way
to drawings or ads from magazines. What might have been

eighth notes floated above maps or rambling prayers
and then staves appeared with no notes at all—

this was the work he'd curse me for disturbing!
The night before his funeral, I sorted through

those composition books and found no sustained melody—
But what did I expect? When he worked, he had a ritual

of rolling up his shirt sleeves and pant legs
that took hours, interrupted by his voices. He'd start

drawing in the margins and press inward, filling each space,
singing to himself like a boy. Oh, he was more selfish

than a child, incapable of loving anyone. I never told him
I wasn't married. I took care of him thirty years, longer

than most marriages last! Such a strange, ugly fellow—
yellow fingered and warp nailed—our one-man Renaissance.

He'd consume his week's supply of pencils in three days,
then beg for more—against the doctor's orders I gave them.

His *March* was signed, "St. Adolf, Chief Music Director,
Painter, Writer, Inventor of 160 Highly Valuable Inventions,

Victor of Mammoth Battles, Alright!! Giant-Theatre-Director,
Great God, Mental Patient, Casualty."

In some ways I was relieved when he died, as if a blizzard
finally howled away and I could start to shovel out.

He didn't want to leave a few perfect works behind him.
He wanted to lift up everything, wanted to give

the whole dying world lasting form.
There were lucid moments when he knew he was mad—

he could almost imagine what a normal life might be.
I'd go home and practice piano every night.

I'd play Beethoven, feel the moments things caught fire,
but couldn't myself become flame.

Page upon page of his *March*, containing, he said, everything
and everyone he'd ever loved, and not a single tune

I could play for his funeral. Not even the *Santa Lisa Polka*.
We buried him without music. There is nothing

I blame myself for more. We buried him without music
and for two weeks I took to bed. Then one night—

it was snowing—I rolled up the sleeves of my nightdress.
I pinned up the hem, then puzzled over a line of music

that vanished in a field of painted irises, purple flags
instead of notes waving under a sky of sharps and flats.

I closed my eyes and began to play. I didn't know
what my hands were doing. Snow kept falling,

silences tumbled forward, winged notes soared
above the chipped ivory keys. I played what I could

of his *Funeral March*—imperfectly, of course,
only in fragments—I played the *Funeral March*

of Adolf Wölfli, everything dark, falling, silver.

Falling from the Grand Hotel

Plunging through staves of music
Adolf Wölfli falls from his Grand Hotel—
in drawing after drawing the haloed figure

plummets to the cobblestones
and is resurrected. Wölfli called this series
The Night of Great Brightness,

returning obsessively to the one fixed point
in his life, his "Highly Special Fatal-Fall."
Twenty years in the schizophrenic ward,

then a field trip: on his first ride in an automobile
Wölfli peeked out to see how everything close-up
blurred as it sped past. In Berne, he knew

each street, pointed out the limestone house
he'd once shared with two hundred goddesses.
Everything just as he remembered

until they reached Cathedral Square
which Wölfli called *The Place of the Resurrection:*
detail after detail, exactly as he'd drawn it,

only without the St. Adolf Grand Hotel.
In its place, more of the city's medieval arcades,
bright colors flattened in midday sun.

But how could a hundred-story giant
disappear? From what had Wölfli fallen?
In the busy square he stood like one

trying to right himself during free fall.
I'm a damned fool, he said finally.
He reached toward his nurse, told her

You're right, I'm an endless dead end.
The breakthrough his nurse hoped for
never came: in the last room of the exhibition

St. Adolf continues to lose his balance.
Wölfli wrote on one self-portrait
God's own voice told me there's nothing

but this falling. We'll fall from anywhere.
If there wasn't a grand hotel
I'd have fallen from a footstool.

Set Design for the City

For David Dawson

Each year, when one end of the football field
was transformed into an opera set, my friend's father—
a chamber musician—played viola in the orchestra,
his annual concession, he said, to bombast.

The summer I was fourteen I went with them
to rehearsals for *Aida*. With the first
updraft of strings I closed my eyes,
saw oblique streets climb through a walled city.

A girl with a leopard showed me a footpath
lined with lady's-slippers and poppies,
smooth petals sliding against us
as we ascended to her garden baths.

The singers, knowing they could look ahead only
to separation and death, lingered
in this hill town, unwilling to leave
through any of its seven gates.

The night of the opera I compared my set
with the arch of Thebes a chorus of slaves
lugged into place and the temple
the conductor seemed to summon from the turf

as the king's retinue approached on weary elephants.
Splendid, all of it, but uninhabitably grand:
I longed for my intimate hanging gardens
where orchids rustled over perfumed water.

One night that summer, after we knew my friend's father
was dying, we listened from our beds
as he practiced Beethoven, rehearsing as if one last concert
had not been canceled. I imagined his eyes

closed, head bent down over his bow,
performing in a twilight garden—
a place of fountains just inside the city walls,
colors softening into blues, hills, night.

But when I woke later and found him still playing
I was in the presence of something too wild
to fit into my imagined city. Watching from the stairs,
I saw how he had stripped to his waist—

playing without a score, he assaulted
each phrase so savagely that at times
the notes could no longer be heard, pressed up
into whatever country he alone fashioned.

The Angels of Bloomington

One of the angels of my childhood
has been restored so well you cannot
see the damage. From the stairs

of Monroe County's museum,
while no one's looking, I run my hand
over smooth limestone wings,

feel where the hammer blows
have been repaired. There used to be
twelve angels. The Egyptian wife

of our Episcopal priest fell in love
with their sculptor. Installation
by installation she transformed

the rectory garden into Paradise.
Older children dared me to run through
the dark yard, touch each frozen giant.

Fierce and sword-wielding, those angels
haunted me for years, especially
in high school after the priest's wife

battered them with a hammer. I recall
stealing into that backyard sanctuary
to see the wreckage with Jana,

one of those intense, brief shots
at loving someone. Whatever compelled us
to those fragments, whatever made us

take our few moments of violent kisses
beneath those broken wings
I miss now in this restoration.

Wanting the cracks to show,
both the love and violence
of the priest's wife. Wanting

the resurrection of the splintered
as much as the whole,
her hammer marks on the limestone sword.

After Reading about an Act of Vandalism in Norwich, Connecticut, My Wife and I Enter Salvatore Verdi's "Bathtub Grotto"

We wanted to see the destruction. We wanted
    to see the broken nose of the Madonna,
wings lying at the feet of angels, Christ

    separated from his cross. Moonlight
on twenty-four white tubs planted vertically
    in the hillside, shrines where the no longer

identical faces of two dozen Marys kept watch
    over the river and North Main Street.
We wanted to imagine what this "Sanctuary of Love"

    looked like yesterday,
twenty years of one man laboring in his backyard because of
    promptings he heard at night. Balanced

with the thrill of someone swinging a hammer
    in the face
of anything that speaks the language *Thou Shalt Not.*

    We found chunks of blue-green glass, slag
from the thermos plant's furnace
    set like emeralds into the Cave of the Nativity.

Joseph, armless, over the fragments of his wife and child.
    By the glow of tiny, colored lights that lined
each of the hill's seven terraces, we made out

    Verdi's latest commentary,
block letters gouged in wet cement:
    GOD HAS CORRECTED MY WORK.

At the summit, at the foot of the cross, we gazed down
　　　at dark windows—Butch's Luncheonette,
Shetucket Plumbing, and the cinder block, silent house

　　　where Verdi lives. Flowing robes
of three battered seraphim in the night wind.
　　　The shard we took from an angel's

fluted, concrete skirt. For days now, we've failed
　　　to find a place for it in our home.

Everyday Books and Cafe

This morning, waiting for the bookstore-cafe to open,
we walked Willimantic's footbridge,
read the spray-paint names of lovers,
each vow partly covering the last:
Carlos and Donna, 1993, Francie and Tito forever, 3-8-94,

the layered names like an undisturbed site
in the archeology of promises.
Beneath us, brown water ran in place, or seemed to,
working out the turbulent marriage
of what's passing and what lasts.

Now I'm warming hands and throat with coffee
while you read outloud from an essay on Blake, follow
the boy on his walk where he sees a tree full of angels,
"their bright wings bespangling the boughs like stars."
Across the street in light snow

two teenagers meet at the bridge, and I imagine
how one of Blake's angels leans forward,
watches these kids join hands.
Perhaps permanence belongs to angelic realms
and all we can hope for here is what recurs. If there are

angels, they might have watched from the bridge, earlier,
as Alison arrived at the store,
named the way she fumbled with her keys "Morning."
But for now, let's share the purely earthly joy
of hearing the same Sarah Vaughn tape

they played here last week, how the waitress
sings along behind the counter.
If we don't let on we know, maybe she'll keep singing,

the teens at the bridge will keep feeding each other
from a paper bag, and at the end of the song Alison

will flip the tape over, play the whole thing again.
And when the couples declare themselves in neon,
promise faithfulness above the rush of the Willimantic,
I think they, like us, just want happiness to last
a little longer, catch and sustain at least

one night's brilliance in the hope and dazzle of day-glow.

Spiritual Direction

Because she poked fun at the way his white robes
flew out behind him as he biked back
to the monastery for vespers

and then, recording her jokes in his journal,
he tried to recall each thing she'd said or done.

Because his hands shook when he phoned her
and later, when they walked beyond the gatehouse,
how the hills wouldn't stop trembling—

he told himself he knew at least this much,
if the world shakes, pay attention!

Because of the long night, then, when he couldn't not
think of her. Or the energy surging
through his ordered life, a wind

rising within him, the same energy he'd followed
long ago into the abbey, almost helpless again before it.

His reaching out of bed for his journal,
trying to describe the sound of her laughter
in the gatehouse corridor. As if God was leading him

away from church, away even from God.
As if he was at last at the mercy.

The Wanderer King

For Annie

1970, Berlin, trying to read Kafka in German.
Tired of traveling, we stayed in bed
all morning, a few blocks from the house
on Grunewaldstrasse where Franz at last defied
his parents, moved in with nineteen-year-old Dora.
The Kafka of my journals longed for books that don't
make us feel good, that *wound*
and stab us, books that might be
the axe for the frozen sea inside us.
But now, reading your journals, Annie, I meet again
the Kafka grateful for two months without demons.
Soon, of course, they would track him down—
someone's always there to tip off demons—
but in Berlin he felt a sweetness almost in reach.

2.

In Berlin, their landlady complained
Franz wrote all night, wasting electricity.
There were strikes in the city,
bread lines and riots, yet you
thought Kafka never happier
than in that last autumn of his life.
You note their plans for a restaurant in Palestine—
Dora, who had just learned to boil water,
would cook; Franz mimed his future role as waiter,
pretending, hands full, to balance
on the bridge of his nose a jug of wine.
Impossible, he conceded, *but why not?*
In Tel Aviv, all restaurants
are run by couples like ourselves.

3.

Like ourselves, they lingered in bed,
each morning collaborating on letters
to a girl whom Kafka had met on a walk,
weeping for her lost doll.
He'd bent over the grieving girl,
tried to comfort her, told her
Your doll is not lost, but traveling.
She was summoned by the Wanderer King
and had to leave at once. When I met her
on the train, just minutes ago,
she promised to write you daily.
Only two sentences in the biography,
so together we tried to imagine
the letters a child received from Kafka.

4.

Children playing a game called Block-the-Road
stop the doll on the outskirts of town.
They joke about her travels, ask endless questions,
then form pyramids, barring the road.
The children keep climbing and falling,
their sunlit faces dazzling before a line
of blackening clouds. Because she's a doll,
she can never tell this world from the next,
thinks these acrobats angels, struggling
to regain heaven. The Wanderer King
continues to elude her. The doll's muslin thins.
When she wavers, wants to return to the girl,
a huge hound seizes the doll by the back
of her neck, carries her farther on her journey.

5.

Caressing her neck, Kafka lies in bed with Dora
all morning, reading the psalms in Hebrew.
From their windows they watch jays hang upside down
from heavy sunflowers, tugging at the last
fat, striped seeds. On the rooftops, pigeons
walk their shadows across brilliant gold tiles.
Sunlight, too, on the spirit stove where last night
they burned two months of Franz's stories and journals.
Because he was in love with words that were
angels or devils, able to raise up or cast down;
because more than once those words
had harmed the ones he loved; because they hoped
to free him to write parables and psalms,
they offered all his notebooks to the flames.

6.

In Kafka's dream, the girl, standing by the flames,
explains *There never was a doll.*
When you found me crying
I made up the story of losing her,
not wanting to tell you I'd been beaten
for lying. The wireless played Brahms
as the girl's home burned. Kafka woke, humming
the bleak melody that played above the blaze.
Remember this, he'd told her, *this is your childhood*
vanishing. The girl, amused, stepped into the rising
spirals of fire. In her white nightgown
she crossed to the crackling bookshelf
where the letters nestled in her china swan-box.
There never was a doll. She writes me every day.

7.

Every day for three weeks a new letter.
Franz in a playful mood at breakfast,
seeking the right end for the doll's story.
Dora consults their proverb calendar,
reads for the twelfth day of October
Even a blind dog finds something sometimes.
One last letter, they decide, relating
the doll's wedding to the Wanderer King.
Brushing Dora's black hair, Franz says
the Wanderer King finds marriage absurd,
one moment's promise binding us
for a lifetime. For Kafka and ourselves
that was the attraction, its unreasonableness,
risking everything on a word.

NOTES

"Letter to Suvorin": This letter is an invention that draws on Anton Chekhov's *The Island of Sakhalin*, a letter to his sister, and several biographies. Alexey Suvorin, Chekhov's publisher and friend, opposed Chekhov's trip to study conditions on the Siberian penal island and refused in advance to publish any book Chekhov wrote on Sakhalin.

"Jacob Stern, Photographer and AIDS Activist, 13th Precinct Station, Manhattan, January 1, 1994": See photo in *Life*, August 11, 1941, pp. 28–29.

"The Wish to See Cyclones": Italicized lines are from Lynda Hull's poem "Lost Fugue for Chet Baker," *Star Ledger* (University of Iowa Press, 1991).

"Rita Machado": Fernando Ramos da Silva (1969–1987) played the title role of Pixote in the 1981 film directed by Hector Babenco. Six years after completing the film, he was killed by police.

"The *Funeral March* of Adolf Wölfli": Adolf Wölfli (1864–1930), schizophrenic painter, composer, and poet who lived most of his life in the Waldau psychiatric hospital near Berne, Switzerland. During his lifetime, Wölfli's musical notations were thought to be merely decorations for his paintings. In recent years, however, some of the music Wölfli first played on rolled-paper trumpets has been deciphered and performed.

ABOUT THE AUTHOR

Michael McAndrews
The Hartford Courant

Born in Duluth, Minnesota, in 1950, Theodore Robert Deppe lives in Florence, Massachusetts, with his wife and three children. His first book, *Children of the Air,* was published by Alice James Books in 1990, and his work has appeared in many journals, including *Poetry, The Kenyon Review,* and *Harper's Magazine.* Winner of an NEA fellowship, a grant from the Connecticut Commission on the Arts, and a full fellowship from the Vermont Studio Center, Deppe is a graduate of Vermont College's MFA in Writing program and holds degrees from Earlham and Berea Colleges. He works as a registered nurse and teaches poetry in a high school for the arts.

RECENT TITLES FROM ALICE JAMES BOOKS

Forrest Hamer, *Call and Response*
E.J. Miller Laino, *Girl Hurt*
Doug Anderson, *The Moon Reflected Fire*
Deborah DeNicola, *Where Divinity Begins*
Richard McCann, *Ghost Letters*
Rita Gabis, *The Wild Field*
Suzanne Matson, *Durable Goods*
David Williams, *Traveling Mercies*
Margaret Lloyd, *This Particular Earthly Scene*
Timothy Liu, *Vox Angelica*
Alice Jones, *The Knot*
Jean Valentine, *The River at Wolf*

Alice James Books has been publishing poetry since 1973. One of
the few presses in the country that is run collectively, the cooperative
selects manuscripts for publication through competitions. New
authors become active members of the press, participating in editorial
and production activities. The press, which places an emphasis on
publishing women poets, was named for Alice James, sister of
William and Henry, whose gift for writing was ignored and whose
fine journal did not appear until after her death.